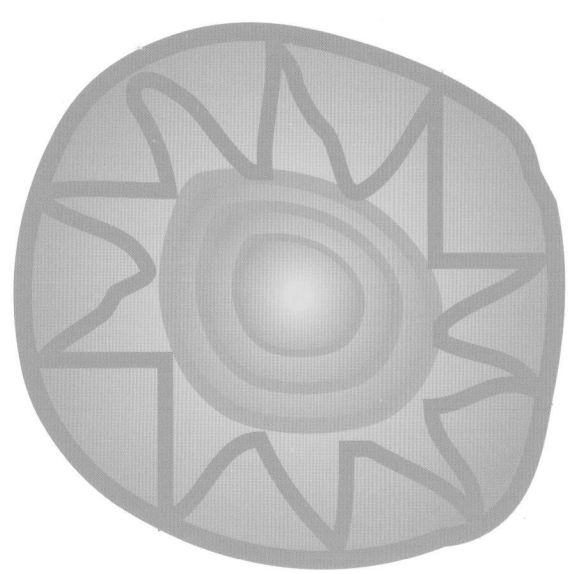

THE
CHUMASH
THROUGH A CHILD'S EYES

BY JOHN WILCOX
ILLUSTRATIONS BY KATE YARBROUGH

ELLIS PARKER SCHOOL

Camas Ridge Library
1150 E. 29th Ave.
Eugene, OR 97403
541-687-3286

for Gertrude, who said that everything would be okay, and especially
for my family and friends who made sure it was.

ACKNOWLEDGMENTS

I would like to take the opportunity to extend my gratitude to the following people:
Jan Timbrook—for lending her valuable time to help in the editing process and for writing the forward;
The library staff at the Santa Barbara Museum of Natural History—for being so helpful;
The Santa Barbara Museum of Natural History—for existing;
The illustrious Monica Weisblott—for her beautiful reference photographs;
Elvia Campos—for lending photographic reference;
Doctors Mayer, Revlin and Johnson—for taking time to look over the book and allowing us to print their kind words;
The staff of McKinley Elementary School—for lending their support,
especially Diane Roth and those who called Michael to tell him they thought the idea was worthwhile;
Jeanne DuPont—for being there in the beginning to bounce off ideas;
To all my friends and family—for their continuous support;
My beautiful, multicultural guru—my wife Rosemarie;
and an extra special thank you to Kate Yarbrough—for her willingness to put up with the
numerous corrections, and without whose artistic expertise this book would not be what it is.

Copyright © 1997, By John Wilcox
All rights reserved.
Printed in Hong Kong

Design, illustration and typography by Kate Yarbrough
Published by Shoreline Press
P.O. Box 3562
Santa Barbara, CA 93130
(805) 687-8340

No part of this book may be used or reproduced without written permission

FOREWORD

American Indian life and culture hold a unique fascination for many people today, and the interest is growing all the time. Nowhere is this more evident than in the Santa Barbara area. More fingerprint smudges are found on the windows of the Chumash Indian village dioramas than on any other exhibits at our museum. Schools reserve all available time slots for docent led tours and talks about the Chumash months in advance. Other Chumash-oriented programs for children and adults are guaranteed hits. Any books about the Chumash fly off the shelves, and requests for more information deluge libraries and curators. All of this is evidence of a widespread and deeply-felt need to understand those who lived here for thousands of years before we came on the scene.

Research is continuing, and every day we learn more about this rich, complex native culture. Scholarly publications are legion, but books about the Chumash for a general audience are still fairly scarce. Many popular books, especially those intended for children, have given priority to appearance over accuracy. This is a special concern for Chumash people today, who want their culture's story portrayed truthfully. *The Chumash Through a Child's Eyes* is proof that style need not sacrifice substance, and that scientifically correct information can be presented in an understandable, interesting way even for very young children.

While presenting their subject with a charming simplicity, author John Wilcox and illustrator Kate Yarbrough have taken meticulous care to depict the principal features of Chumash daily life before the mission period as accurately as possible. From house shapes, basket designs and games, to food gathering, cooking and cave painting, every aspect of both text and drawings has been carefully reviewed to make sure it reflects current anthropological knowledge. This delightful book opens a window into the past for young readers and will help them to understand that, despite our many differences, all the world's people are really much the same.

—Jan Timbrook
Senior Associate Curator of Anthropology
Santa Barbara Museum of Natural History

I awoke this morning to the usual sounds.

The Chumash used a bowl, called a mortar, with a pestle to grind their food. Seeds, vegetables, and sometimes meat were ground before eating. The mortar and pestle were usually made from sandstone.

As I ate breakfast, I thought about what to do today.

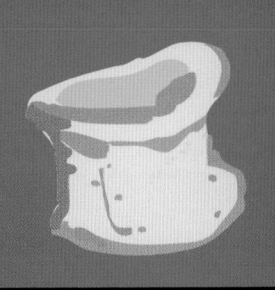

Sometimes the vertebra, one of the backbones, from a whale was used as a stool. Circular pieces of wood were also used for this purpose.

The Chumash kept dogs as pets, to guard against strangers, and to help in hunting.

My mother might want help with the cooking.

In order to cook acorn flour, it was put into a cooking basket with water. Then , a stone was heated on a fire and placed into the basket. The hot stone made the liquid boil quickly and begin to thicken. When the stone was pulled out of the basket, some acorn mush would be cooked onto it. These "chips" were a great treat for mom's helper.

But, first, I will have to get the food.

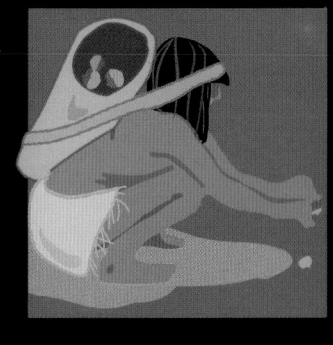

This is a type of basket that was used to carry nuts and berries that the Chumash gathered. With the wide opening, a handful could be dropped over the shoulder into the basket.

Before they were used, the acorns would be stored for a few months to dry out.

I could go fishing.

Two children splash the water to scare the fish. The fish then swim into the waiting net. The Chumash also used fish hooks and harpoons to catch fish.

Maybe I will take a bath.

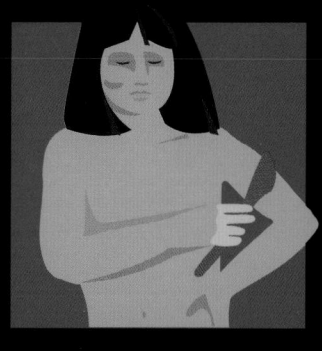

During a bath in the sweathouse, a dolphin jawbone was often used to scrape away the dirt and sweat. Afterwards, it was common to jump into the ocean or a nearby stream to rinse off.

I could help my father work on the house.

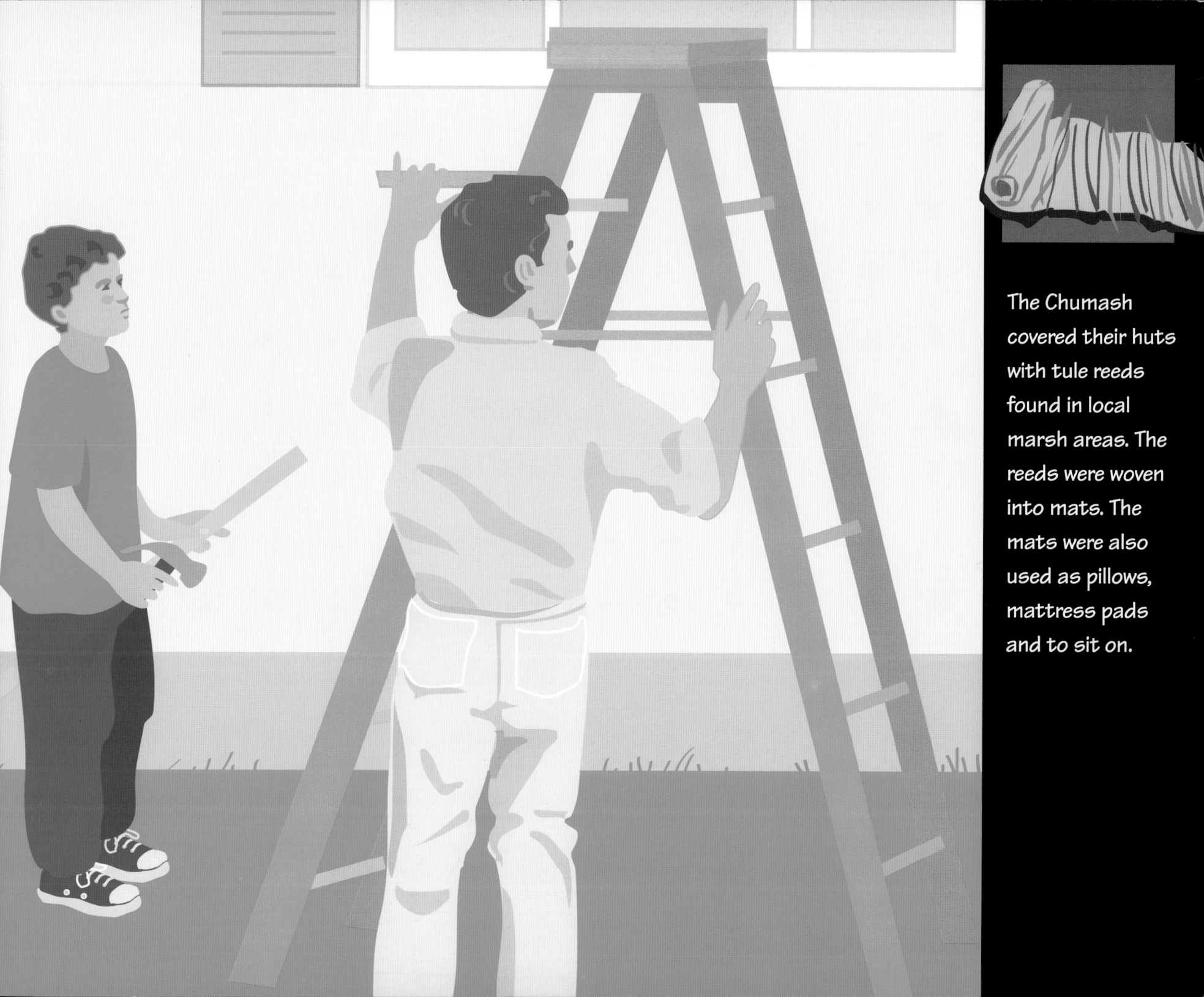

The Chumash covered their huts with tule reeds found in local marsh areas. The reeds were woven into mats. The mats were also used as pillows, mattress pads and to sit on.

Or, we could work on the boat.

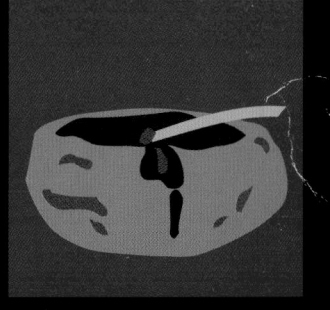

The Chumash word for the canoes they made is tomol. The making of tomols was a very special art done by men. A mixture of tar and pine pitch was used to help hold the planks together and to patch any holes.

But, my father might be busy painting.

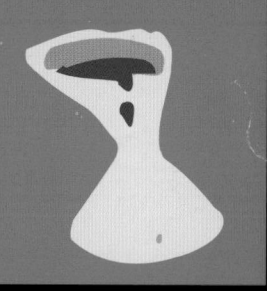

The Chumash made pigments by grinding natural materials into a powder. The powder would then be mixed with water or oil to form paint.

Sometimes a section of vertebra from a swordfish was hollowed out partially and used to hold the paint.

The Chumash paintings were meant to be private. They were probably a form of spiritual or religious expression.

My sister is feeling sick.

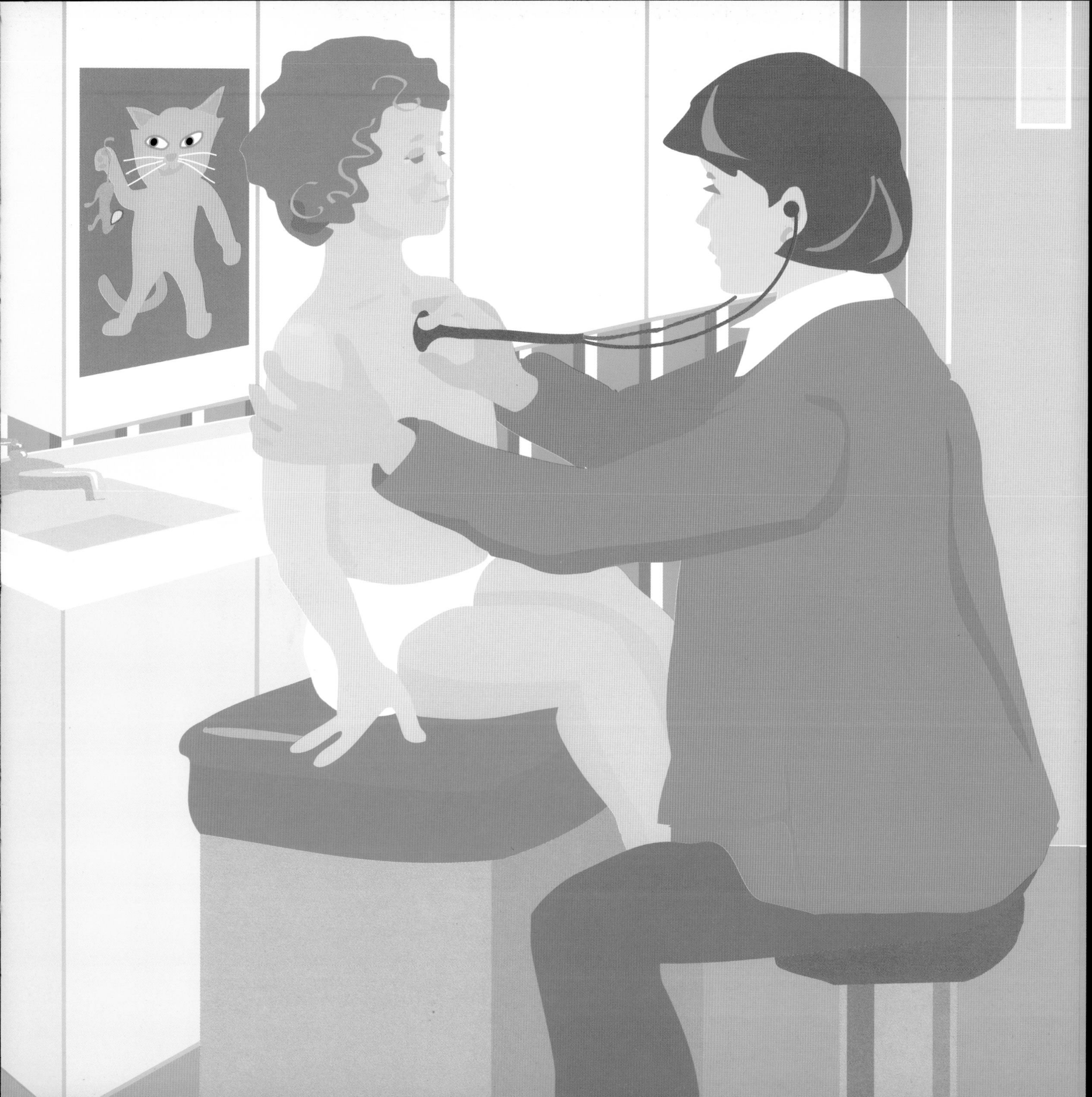

Cups made from a green stone (steatite) were used to drink tea from when one was sick. Teas were made from various plants chosen to cure certain ailments.

The doctor, or shaman would sometimes use a pipe to "blow away" the illness.

Maybe I will play games with my friends.

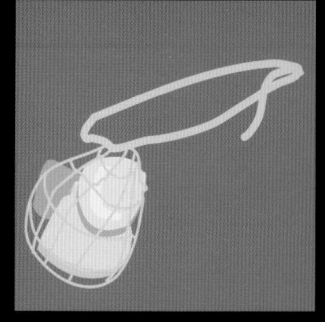

Nets were tied to a belt to carry tools, shells, food, and other objects. The nets were made from woven plant fibers.

Shells were used as bowls, spoons, and as a digging tool.

The Chumash played archery games, marbles, kickball, and a hockey-like game called shinny.

I hope we can go swimming.

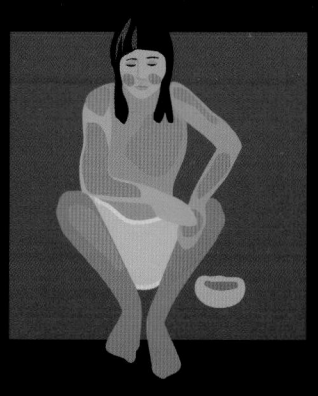

The Chumash made a paste using the mineral hematite (iron oxide) that they would rub upon themselves. This red-colored sun-screen worked well.

I could listen to music with my friends.

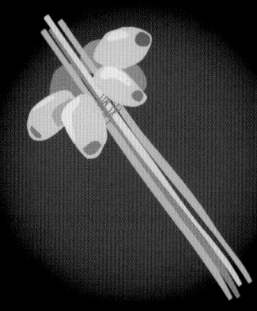

The Chumash used a variety of objects found in their environment to make musical instruments. This rattle was made by filling moth cocoons with pebbles. The cocoons were then tied to sticks that were bound together.

But, I think that for now I will just find a place to relax by myself.

JOHN WILCOX is a native Santa Barbaran. He has recently
earned his multiple-subject credential and plans on
staying in the area to teach. John lives in Goleta, California
with his wife Rosemarie and their dogs and cats.
This is his first published work.

KATE YARBROUGH is a designer and illustrator who works
in many media and has recently developed an interest
in children's books. She lives in Santa Barbara.